The Good Gift Giver

21 Days of
Unexpected Blessings

TAHNI CULLEN,
JOSIAH CULLEN,
and CHERYL RICKER

BroadStreet
P U B L I S H I N G

BroadStreet Publishing Group, LLC
Racine, Wisconsin, USA
BroadStreetPublishing.com

The Good Gift Giver: 21 Days of Unexpected Blessings

Copyright © 2017 Tahni Cullen and Cheryl Ricker

ISBN-13: 978-1-4245-5479-9 (softcover)
ISBN-13: 978-1-4245-5483-6 (e-book)

Stock or custom editions of BroadStreet Publishing titles may be purchased in bulk for educational, business, ministry, fundraising, or sales promotional use. For information, please e-mail info@broadstreetpublishing.com.

Cover design by Chris Garborg at garborgdesign.com
Interior design and typeset by Katherine Lloyd at theDESKonline.com

Printed in the United States of America

17 18 19 20 21 5 4 3 2 1

The
Good Gift
Giver

Contents

The Good Gift Giver

By Tahni Cullen

M y life spun me into "supernatural mode" when my seven-year-old, nonverbal, and autistic son, Josiah, who had never been traditionally taught to read or write, suddenly typed his first independent sentence on an iPad: *God is a good gift giver.*

God unlocked my son's spiritual senses to the deep joys of heaven, renewing my hope, joy, and excitement for God's Word, power, and presence. Josiah's gems on our Josiah's Fire Facebook page delight people from around the world with his wisdom, insight, and hope.

What a joy to partner with my dear friend, Cheryl Ricker, writer and coauthor of *Josiah's Fire: Autism Stole His Words, God Gave Him a Voice.* As we share Josiah's quotes with twenty-one personal devotionals, we know they will spark fresh gratitude for gifts you have not even yet identified—

gifts personally prepared for you by the good Gift Giver himself.

James 1:17 says, "Every good and perfect gift is from above, coming down from the Father of the heavenly lights, who does not change like shifting shadows" (NIV).

The Good Gift Giver

God is a good gift giver . . .
If faith, then he gives it.
If joy, he finds it for you.
If love, he names it to you.
If hindsight, he recalls it to you.
If boldness, he joins it to you.
If diligence, he brings it to you.
If peace, he sends it to you.
If wisdom, he teaches it to you.
If hope, he presents it to you.
If thankfulness, he plants it in you.
If joy, he builds it into time for you.
Open it as freshly as you can.

—*Josiah Cullen*

Does a trout get banged up if swimming upstream? Reasonable fish tell you to go with the flow, but a trout hangs on his every instinct to love upstream.

—Josiah Cullen

DAY 1

Against the Current

By Tahni Cullen

Jesus said, "In this world you will have trouble" (John 16:33 NIV). So why do we struggle so much when trouble strikes? Where did God go?

When the Father opened Josiah's communication through typing, I thought we would finally be free of the intense pressure autism had brought into our lives for five years. Surely healing would come and bring us back to the easy life God intended.

But what if the journey of a God seeker unfolds differently? Although I continue to pray expectantly for Josiah's wholeness, God uses him and his words to uniquely show me how I perceive my life through distorted goggles and that we can always overcome because Jesus overcame for us!

I didn't know anything about trout when Josiah first wrote about them on the iPad, but it turns out that when it's time for them to birth upstream, these creatures are designed to do impossible feats to overcome the most impassible areas. Neither the strength of the current, nor the size of the rocks, nor the power of crashing waterfalls can keep a breathing trout from reaching its destiny.

Will you let resistance keep you from yours?

Meditation

> I'm not asking you to take them out of the world, but to keep them safe from the evil one. (John 17:15 NLT)

> For he raised us from the dead along with Christ and seated us with him in the heavenly realms because we are united with Christ Jesus. (Ephesians 2:6 NLT)

> No, in all these things we are more than conquerors through him who loved us. For I am convinced that neither death nor life, neither angels nor demons, neither the present nor the future, nor any powers, neither height nor depth, nor anything else in all creation, will be able to separate us from the love of God that is in Christ Jesus our Lord. (Romans 8:37–39 NIV)

Reflection

What's an example of resistance that you have faced or are now facing? How do those times impact your relationship with God?

Journal

Journal

Faith is believing for kites to fly when there's no wind in sight.

—Josiah Cullen

DAY 2

Positive Positioning

By Cheryl Ricker

Has God ever asked you to do something unreasonable? This happened to me when God whispered to my nine-year-old heart that someday he wanted me to write books for his glory. How could I do that when my teacher had placed me in remedial reading with foreigners who didn't even speak English?

But since when does God get nervous about our insecurity or immaturity? Even our momentary natural limits don't have the power to stop the one who has a history of using unlikely vessels to do great things.

God used weak and fearful people like Gideon to defeat massive Midianite armies. Gideon could have enlisted support from tens of thousands of soldiers, but God wanted to whittle it down to a measly three hundred to pull off the impossible.

Likewise, God enjoyed personally teaching, leading, and developing me, helping me against the odds to write and publish several books that happen to highlight his goodness.

When tempted to fret over impossible-looking circumstances, why not call on the miracle-working breeze-maker who loves making things fly for his glory?

Papa, thank you for calling unlikely people and infusing weakness with your strength to showcase your glory on earth as it is in heaven.

Meditation

> Now faith is confidence in what we hope for and assurance about what we do not see. (Hebrews 11:1 NIV)

> "My thoughts are nothing like your thoughts," says the Lord. "And my ways are far beyond anything you could imagine." (Isaiah 55:8 NLT)

> Instead, God chose things the world considers foolish in order to shame those who think they are wise. And he chose things that are powerless to shame those who are powerful. (1 Corinthians 1:27 NLT)

Reflection

*Describe an area in your life where you'd
like to yield more to God's dreams, gifts,
and possibilities even if you don't yet feel the wind.*

Journal

My worth is not a line
to cross when I wake up
each morning. It is actually
a stare down to say,
"I will erase this line
altogether because
I woke up already prized."

—Josiah Cullen

DAY 3

Approval Traps

By Tahni Cullen

Is Father God proud of you?

I spent my elementary years enrolled in a fairly strict Christian school. Five-year-old me quickly learned that my teachers expected swift obedience without question. I tried to be good, win their approval, and dodge those dreaded yellow detention slips.

Shame may have been my school's swift enforcer, but earning awards became my key motivator. Each year I worked and studied hard to edge out the competition and come away with piles of trophies and medals.

I loved hearing the clapping crowd and seeing my teachers beam while I received my accolades. I was an achiever, and I intended to keep it that way. But what happens when, no matter hard you try, you don't win at life? Are you still worthy of approval?

Jesus' disciples knew the amazing feeling of success as they regularly witnessed God's power displayed in and through them. They even argued about which of them was the greatest. Isn't it interesting how excessive shame and excessive praise can trigger the same reaction?

Jesus gently redirected them as he does with us. It's not about coming in first. It's about actions springing from the secure, serving heart of a prized child. Thank God! Our worth isn't based on what we can do, but simply to whom we belong.

Meditation

> See what great love the Father has lavished on us, that we should be called children of God! And that is what we are! (1 John 3:1 NIV)

> For we are God's masterpiece. He has created us anew in Christ Jesus, so we can do the good things he planned for us long ago. (Ephesians 2:10 NLT)

Reflection

> *Write about a time when you were rewarded for achievement. How did it make you feel?*

> *How does Father God feel about you on any given day?*

Journal

Angels turn tears

into minutes

of amens.

—Josiah Cullen

DAY 4

Angels Everywhere

By Cheryl Ricker

Have you ever perceived the presence of angels?

Josiah saw them at the mall, McDonald's, the children's museum, and multiple times at home. Imagine if someone like Josiah woke you up in the middle of the night and described angels standing directly in front of you? Yikes!

Whether or not we see them, they're there. When Peter was imprisoned during Passover, an angel woke him and his chains immediately fell off. The angel told him to put on his clothes, and Peter followed him past the guards and out to the iron gate that opened by itself. Peter walked the full length of the street before realizing he wasn't having a vision.

The church had been praying, and God sent an angel to rescue him.

You may feel too burdened to pray aloud, but the Holy Spirit is big enough to hear your heart's cry and send mighty angels to action. These heavenly beings can line things up, station people in places, and bring us to safety, favor, and spiritual growth.

Imagine how different we'd feel if we stayed aware of angels whose bold actions echo God's "Let it be so!" Knowing we're supernaturally surrounded helps us feel less vulnerable and more pumped about God's plan, which is always for our best anyway.

Meditation

The LORD is close to the brokenhearted;
> he rescues those whose spirits are crushed.

(Psalm 34:18 NLT)

Therefore, angels are only servants—spirits sent to care for people who will inherit salvation.
(Hebrews 1:14 NLT)

Praise the LORD, you angels,
> you mighty ones who carry out his plans,
> listening for each of his commands.

(Psalm 103:20 NLT)

Reflection

> *What might it look like if an angel*
> *were to appear and free you from*
> *one of your current trials?*

Journal

Journal

My piano might hand
me lost keys if my
piano is reframed.

—Josiah Cullen

DAY 5

Mindful Measures

By Tahni Cullen

Most days, my prayers start with a sincere plea: "God, transform me by changing how I think."

As children, we have a natural curiosity and fire out lots of questions. Somewhere along the way, however, society tries to teach us the "right answers," and our minds get set.

Josiah regularly blows my mind with his ready ear tuned to heaven's wisdom. God's thoughts are not our thoughts, and yet he gives us the mind of Christ. Could that be an invitation to think bigger?

Something struck me while pondering Josiah's words about lost piano keys. Could the three-hundred-year-old invention of the eighty-eight key piano exist on a larger scale in heaven? It made sense considering how our eternal home will feature a huge, limitless type of music and instruments. But to even consider the thought, I had to expand and "reframe" my thinking.

Pushing boundaries on things that are already established usually meets some type of mental or social resistance. Perhaps the God who never changes wants to spiritually and naturally reveal more than we dare imagine. Are we willing to make room for it?

Meditation

"Call to Me, and I will answer you, and show you great and mighty things, which you do not know." (Jeremiah 33:3 NKJV)

Now we have received, not the spirit of the world, but the Spirit who is from God, that we might know the things that have been freely given to us by God. These things we also speak, not in words which man's wisdom teaches but which the Holy Spirit teaches, comparing spiritual things with spiritual. (1 Corinthians 2:12–13 NKJV)

Reflection

*Write a prayer asking God to expand
your insight about a spiritual or physical
matter that you're passionate about.
Ask God a few specific questions about it.*

Journal

Loud giants fire off gongs
of hot-tempered hooey.
Just get a stone of praise
and take a giant down
faster than time could fly.

—Josiah Cullen

Giants in the Land

By Cheryl Ricker

Have you ever thought of fear as a perspective problem? One of the many things Tahni and I have in common is we have both struggled with panic attacks while driving. Almost nothing is worse than that heart-pounding, out-of-control feeling of fear, or "peace irrationalized," as Josiah calls it.

After Moses' twelve spies returned from exploring the land flowing with milk and honey, their hearts beat wildly as they warned people of the inhabitants they described as undefeatable giants. "We seemed like grasshoppers in our own eyes, and we looked the same to them," they cried, spreading fear like disease (Numbers 13:33 NIV).

Caleb silenced their hair-raising report in exchange for a different perspective, "We should go up and take possession of the land, for we can certainly do it" (v. 30 NIV). Caleb refused to let fear rob him of God's promises.

Likewise, young David could have feared Goliath and let the Israelites be continually dominated by the enemy; instead, he kept his eyes on the size of his God, turning tyranny to freedom.

Satan appears more giantlike than he really is, roaring like a lion while working up his biggest threat. The best way to silence his lies is to remember God's loving character and fully praise him as he deserves. Praise summons its cousins, confidence and thanksgiving, and it reminds our souls of our true identity.

When we focus on the Prince of Peace, we knock down life's biggest giants and walk in the supernatural victory God has already given us!

Meditation

> Be alert and of sober mind. Your enemy the devil prowls around like a roaring lion looking for someone to devour. Resist him, standing firm in the faith, because you know that the family of believers throughout the world is undergoing the same kind of sufferings. (1 Peter 5:8–9 NIV)

> "The LORD who rescued me from the paw of the lion and the paw of the bear will rescue me from the hand of this Philistine." (1 Samuel 17:37 NIV)

> Why, my soul, are you downcast?
> Why so disturbed within me?
> Put your hope in God,
> for I will yet praise him,
> my Savior and my God. (Psalm 43:5 NIV)

Reflection

> *In light of the giants you are facing*
> *in your life, write a praise that*
> *focuses on the bigness of God.*

Journal

Rehearse gravity and nothing rises. Hope is helium to your lungs. Hope is lighter than air. Traveling fast, it frees itself from failure.

—Josiah Cullen

DAY 7

What's My Line?

By Tahni Cullen

In high school and college, I clocked in many nights at theater rehearsals. I loved the challenge of developing new characters until each line and move turned out just right.

I discovered, however, that actors who learn their lines so well that they can recite them without thinking risk disconnecting from authentic emotion. They may have all the right inflections and tones, but if the delivery is no longer dynamic, they're prone to give a stale performance.

On the stage of life, Jesus instructs us to be intentional about what we say. Whether we speak meaningless, rehearsed prayer repetitions or share exactly what's in our mouths, Jesus warns, "Words are powerful; take them seriously. Words can be your salvation. Words can also be your damnation" (Matthew 12:37 MSG).

The average person complains fifteen to thirty times a day, which totals about fifty-three hours a year of doling out humanity's woes. However, when our minds, hearts, and words connect to the Spirit, the powerful one who is language of life within us, we can change the atmosphere.

Are you ready to speak life and mean it?

Meditation

Then the LORD said to me, "You have seen well, for I am watching over my word to perform it." (Jeremiah 1:12 ESV)

"The good person out of the good treasure of his heart produces good, and the evil person out of his evil treasure produces evil, for out of the abundance of the heart his mouth speaks." (Luke 6:45 ESV)

May the words of my mouth
and the meditation of my heart
be pleasing to you,
O LORD, my rock and my redeemer.
(Psalm 19:14 NLT)

Reflection

*Write a list of your most common verbalized woes.
Then write a list of things you're most
thankful for today. Take twenty-four hours to
openly rehearse talking to God and others
about what you're thankful for.*

Journal

Journal

Water a garden to life
rather than weeding
a garden to death.

—Josiah Cullen

Life Garden

By Cheryl Ricker

Do you water or weed?

It blesses me to watch Tahni invest in Josiah's physical, emotional, and spiritual growth. She's a great example of how to intentionally bring out the best in people.

I messed up on this one when I first got married. In my eager attempts to dutifully weed my husband's precious garden, I failed to see all the ugly weeds cropping up in my own. And I quickly learned that the Holy Spirit does a much better weeding job than I do. His ways lead to peace and life, not death and strife.

In the Apostle Paul's letters to the church, he felt responsible for fellow believers and constantly encouraged them, pouring his best into them. Other times, he challenged them and offered correction, but only in love, staying optimistic, realistic, and hopeful. He desperately wanted to see them step into their destiny in Christ, so he acted like Jesus, who doesn't weed people unless he first douses their souls' soil in his living water.

If you've messed up like I did, don't sweat it, okay? It's never too late to start doing the right thing. When you truly encourage others, you offer refreshing water that brings life. Love like this and watch life spring to your own soul as well.

Meditation

> The generous soul will be made rich,
> And he who waters will also be watered himself.
> (Proverbs 11:25 NKJV)

> "The farmer's workers went to him and said, 'Sir, the field where you planted that good seed is full of weeds! Where did they come from?'
>
> 'An enemy has done this!' the farmer exclaimed. 'Should we pull out the weeds?' they asked. 'No,' he replied, 'you'll uproot the wheat if you do.'" (Matthew 13:27–29 NLT)

> Therefore encourage one another and build each other up, just as in fact you are doing. (1 Thessalonians 5:11 NIV)

Reflection

Who do you want to encourage today?
What could you do or say?

Journal

Goal mining is so big to people, but bright minutes in God's hands are man's best plans.

—Josiah Cullen

DAY 9

Divine Agendas

By Tahni Cullen

For much of my adult career, my work revolved around meeting deadlines and producing quality marketing materials. I oversaw details, dates, and deliveries with precision.

After changing career paths to move into ministry, I learned that people progress isn't nearly as tangible as project progress. How could I tell if my investment in others was making a difference? Spiritual growth and personal improvement don't plot as neatly on a spreadsheet, because people are messy.

During that time, Josiah wasn't on a predictable development path either, but God was doing something behind the scenes. It didn't matter how much I set my long-term goals, because a lot of factors stayed out of my control. But that uncomfortable feeling kept me dependent on God daily.

I began to learn that God's ancient people, the Hebrews, didn't maintain the same Western Greek mindset that everything happens on a linear timeline. Instead, the Jews understood that our lives mirror nature's cycles and seasons. It was enough that God alone held the way of life.

Seeking the Lord's presence through each of life's momentary twists and turns brings fullness of joy. His presence breaks into chaos and grows us—perfectly on time and in season.

Meditation

> Commit your works to the LORD,
> And your thoughts will be established.
> (Proverbs 16:3 NKJV)

> A man's heart plans his way,
> But the LORD directs his steps.
> (Proverbs 16:9 NKJV)

> "If you grow a healthy tree, you'll pick healthy fruit.
> If you grow a diseased tree, you'll pick worm-eaten
> fruit. The fruit tells you about the tree."
> (Matthew 12:33 MSG)

Reflection

> *What's a goal you've approached from*
> *many angles but can't seem to get traction on?*

> *What might God's agenda be for you*
> *during this season of your life?*

Journal

Bold people bash their molds and put themselves on the Potter's wheel.

—Josiah Cullen

DAY 10

Beautiful Submission

By Cheryl Ricker

To some people boldness means leaping into goals with determination and courage, even breaking rules if necessary. But true boldness often requires following God outside of one's comfort zone.

I needed God's boldness when he called me to write supernatural stories, because not all of my family members believe God's gifts are for today. Would I be brave and say yes to the call when I'd likely be judged and misunderstood?

When Mary agreed to be the mother of Jesus, she knew the risks of being misunderstood. She knew she would face hardship and be falsely accused. But this highly favored woman chose to stay on the Potter's wheel instead of taking the easy, more walked-upon path.

Stepping out in grace and dignity, Mary revealed rich character that would later be a compelling example for a young Jesus to follow.

As Jesus grew up, he lived and spoke his Father's truth despite the worst opposition and judgment, and he submitted all the way to the cross.

Since he rose from the dead and gave us his Holy Spirit, Christ empowers us to boldly and confidently stay on his wheel, trusting he'll uniquely grow and shape us in the best possible way until we see him face-to-face.

Meditation

> But the jar he was making did not turn out as he had hoped, so he crushed it into a lump of clay again and started over. (Jeremiah 18:4 NLT)

> But we have this treasure in jars of clay to show that this all-surpassing power is from God and not from us. (2 Corinthians 4:7 NIV)

Reflection

*Share some experiences of either
staying on the wheel or jumping off.*

Journal

Journal

Prayer looks like this:
Open up the pump with
the handle of prayer.
Prime the pump with hope.
Let the water flow
with faith.

—Josiah Cullen

Pray at the Pump

By Tahni Cullen

It's hard to imagine parents putting their eleven-year-old kid behind the wheel of a car, but my mom, Sharon, grew up on a ranch in the 1950s, and that's what they did. Little Sharon got the big responsibility of hauling water from the field pump to the house.

One day she loaded the trunk with aluminum cream cans and headed out. Unfortunately, she misjudged her turn and ran over the pump, damaging the car and the spout. Frightened and frustrated, she abandoned the scene and hid in the outhouse.

If prayer is like getting a working flow of water from a pump, why does it feel so complicated? It's easy to overshoot it or to simply give up on it. We are given this responsibility so we can wield a lot of power, but how do we get comfortable around the fountain of living water?

Holy Spirit as instructor kindly does with us as Sharon's mom did with her. She matter-of-factly said, "I see you ran over the pump. Well, your dad is going into town to get a part for it, and he'll also weld up the car. Tomorrow I'll go back out with you and show you where to turn so you can get water from the pump."

Meditation

I waited and waited and waited for GOD.
At last he looked; finally he listened.
He lifted me out of the ditch,
pulled me from deep mud.
He stood me up on a solid rock
to make sure I wouldn't slip.
He taught me how to sing the latest God-song,
a praise-song to our God.
More and more people are seeing this:
they enter the mystery,
abandoning themselves to GOD.
(Psalm 40:1–3 MSG)

But when the Father sends the Advocate as my representative—that is, the Holy Spirit—he will teach you everything and will remind you of everything I have told you. (John 14:26 NLT)

Reflection

*How would you describe your comfort level
and flow with prayer these days?*

*List three problems
for which you are believing God's solution.*

Journal

Hope is like mail to God
that you would like his
faith in reply.

-Josiah Cullen

DAY 12

Keys and Doors

By Cheryl Ricker

When I lost the remote-control keys to my car and mini-van and asked God to pretty please help me find them, three long weeks went by, and I finally received a call from the manager of Godfather's Pizza, saying someone had found them under a table. Since they had a tag from our car dealership, the manager was able to track me down.

The Godfather's faith-builder incident prepared me for my next dilemma involving the breakdown of the mechanism in my van's automatic sliding door. Knowing the repair would cost a couple thousand dollars we didn't have, I told my family, "There's no other way. God's just going to have to do a miracle." Two days later, we received a notice in the mail for a recall on the door mechanism that matched the same make and model of our broken one.

God came through in a jiffy. Clearly much faster than he did for Abraham. When God promised the seventy-five-year-old man the impossible gift of a son, Abraham knew God was faithful, so for many long years he continued to persevere in hope. Sure enough, Isaac eventually stepped into history in God's perfect time.

When things don't work out, why not rest our hope in the one who hands us the keys, opens the right doors he planned, and increases our faith for whatever comes next?

Meditation

Now faith is the substance of things hoped for, the evidence of things not seen. (Hebrews 11:1 NKJV)

Hope deferred makes the heart sick,
   but a longing fulfilled is a tree of life.
(Proverbs 13:12 NLT)

Reflection

*Write about someone whose hope-filled
journey has inspired you. Ask God to bless them
and make you a similar inspiration to someone else.*

Journal

Miles make you joyful
in the little things
to befriend the
biggest adventures.

—Josiah Cullen

DAY 13

Small Wonders

By Tahni Cullen

Modern wisdom says, "Don't sweat the small stuff," but that doesn't mean we should gloss over small wonder-rich moments.

After I turned forty, it struck me how much my outlook had changed. Strolling in an unfamiliar neighborhood on a misty day, I delighted in little things—a bee in a lone flower, intricate green highlights tinting a shrub, the far-off sound of chimes. Struck by dozens of details, I thanked God for his creativity poking out everywhere.

I remembered back to when Josiah's Rapid Prompting Method communication instructor told me Josiah was an auditory learner. "Speak to him at age level," she said, "but describe everything as if you were talking to someone who was blind."

As I took her advice, outings and walks with Josiah came alive. He didn't always look, but I began overemphasizing things like veins on the leaves or swallows swooping into a distant birdhouse. We no longer hurried to get to the park, and we relished the small things.

Elijah noticed something small as he prayed for rain: a cloud as tiny as a man's hand. He rejoiced in it because it revealed that a God-sized adventure would soon begin.

Are you respecting the signs of small beginnings?

Meditation

> "Do not despise these small beginnings, for the LORD rejoices to see the work begin, to see the plumb line in Zerubbabel's hand." (Zechariah 4:10 NLT)

> He told them another parable: "The kingdom of heaven is like a mustard seed, which a man took and planted in his field. Though it is the smallest of all seeds, yet when it grows, it is the largest of garden plants and becomes a tree, so that the birds come and perch in its branches." (Matthew 13:31–32 NIV)

> Send me a sign of your favor. (Psalm 86:17 NLT)

Reflection

What little things delight you?
Write a prayer asking God to confirm his love
by making you aware of small things
pointing to bigger adventures.

Journal

Journal

Sing like

an overcomer.

—Josiah Cullen

DAY 14

To a Different Tune

By Cheryl Ricker

C an you sing in times of trouble?

When Jehoshaphat, king of Judah, discovered a vast army approaching, defeat looked imminent. Jehoshaphat was a godly king, so he called all of Judah together to remember the good things God had done and to acknowledge God as their only hope.

That's when they did the unthinkable. They sent musicians to the front of their army to sing and to worship God. By the time they reached the opposition, God had already destroyed their enemies, so all Judah's army had left to do was gather the plunder.

Singing has a way of releasing God's people into deeper freedom, and it reminds us that supernatural vision transcends the natural kind.

Even the ability to choose praise is a gift. When stuck in the thick of battle, we simply need to remember Jesus already won. He overcame in death so we can overcome in life. He took on weakness to give us strength.

Whenever we release an overcomer's victory song, we announce before heaven and earth who we are and whose we are. Can you imagine the cloud of witnesses peeking down to watch us joyfully march to heaven's tune?

Meditation

And when he had consulted with the people, he appointed those who should sing to the LORD, and who should praise the beauty of holiness, as they went out before the army and were saying: "Praise the LORD, For His mercy endures forever."
(2 Chronicles 20:21 NKJV)

But I trust in your unfailing love.
I will rejoice because you have rescued me.
I will sing to the LORD
because he is good to me. (Psalm 13:5–6 NLT)

Reflection

*Write a praise-filled song
for you or a friend to declare victory
over an impossible situation.*

Journal

Plan laughter into your life inside of Jesus.

Light your heart in oil.

Appointing lanterns to your silliness is lovely to him.

—Josiah Cullen

DAY 15

Fireflies

By Tahni Cullen

I grew up in the American Great Plains and didn't have the childhood delight of capturing fireflies, which apparently prefer trees and humidity to grass and dry air.

A few years ago, however, while on a summer trip through an Illinois town at sunset, I stopped with my husband, Joe, and Josiah at an enchanted city park. I breathed deeply and admired the whimsical sculptures that dotted the lawn near ponds with playful ducks and swans.

The three of us held hands and strolled down a path canopied by dense trees. We'd gone too far considering the descending darkness and the fact that we didn't know where the path would lead.

"Let's go back," said Joe. But just then, as if on cue, fireflies lit up all around us. They twinkled and synchronized like holiday lights, firing up on one side and responding on the other. I felt my face brighten, sensing God's smile. And like a giddy schoolgirl, I skipped as I pointed out God's tiny creatures to Josiah.

God often hints of his perfect ways through nature. Jesus called us to light up the darkness, and Papa made fireflies that use light to "talk" to one another. He designed them to emit the most efficient light in the world. A fun, brilliant, creative, and unexpected light—like we can be.

Imagine the fun we could have communicating that kind of light to the world!

Meditation

> You love justice and hate evil.
>> Therefore God, your God, has anointed you,
>> pouring out the oil of joy on you more than on
>> anyone else. (Psalm 45:7 NLT)

Here's another way to put it: You're here to be light, bringing out the God-colors in the world. (Matthew 5:14 MSG)

> Those who look to him for help will be radiant
>> with joy;
> no shadow of shame will darken their faces.
> (Psalm 34:5 NLT)

Reflection

How has God used an example from
nature to trigger a provoking thought
or a moment of joy for you?
What sort of things are you most
surprisingly delighted by?

Journal

Jobs take time, but pearls take miracles to form. A round pearl is troubling to you only if trouble does not leave your shell in beauty.

—Josiah Cullen

DAY 16

Patience in Trouble

By Cheryl Ricker

A natural pearl is formed when an irritant, usually a parasite, enters a shell. Over a period of years, the clam secretes fluid called "nacre" that coats the irritant in multiple layers until the pearl is complete.

Supernatural surprises emerged while Tahni and I worked on *Josiah's Fire*. At the start of the first chapter, God gave me a metaphor of a bomb exploding to describe the trouble closing in on the Cullen family. At that point I had no idea Josiah would later write about God's love being stronger than a bomb and give us a zinger of a quote for the book's ending.

Isn't that just like God to perfect things in his time with the best possible ending in mind?

Even when life's irritants and parasites start to get to us, the Holy Spirit is more than capable of coating each detail of our lives with his "nacre" goodness. We are only "troubled" when we remove the pearl from its shell before its time.

Since we're all in process, we need to give others and ourselves grace and patience. When we give God time and room to form miracles, we can rejoice that he will pour his beauty in and through each of us, his pearls.

Meditation

> I have seen the God-given task with which the sons of men are to be occupied. He has made everything beautiful in its time. Also He has put eternity in their hearts, except that no one can find out the work that God does from beginning to end. (Ecclesiastes 3:10–11 NKJV)

> Again, the kingdom of heaven is like a merchant seeking beautiful pearls, who, when he had found one pearl of great price, went and sold all that he had and bought it. (Matthew 13:45–46 NKJV)

Reflection

Name some irritants in your life that later produced beauty. Did you feel like giving up while waiting? How did the Holy Spirit coat the situation with goodness while you waited?

Journal

Journal

Love is Light,

asked for and given

without borders.

—Josiah Cullen

Beyond Borders

By Tahni Cullen

"God so loves the Pangea," Josiah typed on the iPad.

"Pangea?" I said, unsure what that was.

Meaning "whole earth," Pangea is the name for all assembled land masses. In Genesis 10:25 and chapter 11, we learn of humanity being scattered across the world. With seven thousand distinct languages now spoken on seven continents, we are divided in countless ways.

The cross, however, reunites us to God and each other.

How inconceivable to imagine erasing all the lines we draw between us—cultural, geographical, political, social, economic, and religious. But envisioning the open-armed Father who wants us all to come home makes you want to try.

When Cheryl and I visited the Witch's Hat Tower landmark, a location for one of the scenes in *Josiah's Fire*, we encountered a group of young people who were definitely outside of our Christian circles. Sensing God's unconditional love, we found ourselves lavishing them with time, encouragement, and a gift. Ever since God amazed us that day, we continued to spur each other on to the extravagant love God exudes for everyone.

In these days of division, we need to keep our antennas up, because you just never know whose walls God might lead us to break through next.

Meditation

> For God did not send his Son into the world to condemn the world, but to save the world through him. (John 3:17 NIV)

> For Christ himself has brought peace to us. He united Jews and Gentiles into one people when, in his own body on the cross, he broke down the wall of hostility that separated us. (Ephesians 2:14 NLT)

> And they sang a new song, saying:
> "You are worthy to take the scroll
>   and to open its seals,
> because you were slain,
>   and with your blood you purchased for God
>   persons from every tribe and language and people
> and nation." (Revelation 5:9 NIV)

Reflection

*What are some conditions you tend to place
on loving others, especially those outside of your
normal community? What's one way you can extend
God's love beyond your typical borders this week?*

Journal

Raid not the man's treasure
next to you, but yours.
Argue sameness if you wish,
but Father made you for more.
Face your nature and wade
into your real self.
You are an original and
there's no one like you.

—Josiah Cullen

DAY 18

Radically Different

By Cheryl Ricker

When I was a child, my family tossed around the word *different* like it was something you definitely didn't want to be. Problem was, I already felt different, both in my family and at school. On good days, "different" meant making jokes with strangers in the candy store. On bad days, however, it meant not fitting in with the popular kids, comparing myself to others, and feeling withdrawn and less than.

As I grew up, I began to see myself as a unique child of the King, and I cherished "different." I took on side jobs as a professional clown, both in town and on mission trips, and I even made peace with a snort I developed along the way—except when it slipped out in church.

The Old Testament prophet Ezekiel did many strange

things that raised a lot of eyebrows, but he also experienced and recorded visions of heaven that revealed the majesty of our Creator.

When Josiah wrote, "sameness is not me," he recognized that God has a good reason for not making duplicates. The Lord wants each of us to find our true self so we can celebrate each little talent, quirk, and streak of color he placed inside us.

Meditation

You saw me before I was born.

Every day of my life was recorded in your book.
Every moment was laid out

before a single day had passed.
How precious are your thoughts about me, O God.

They cannot be numbered! (Psalm 139:16–18 NLT)

In his grace, God has given us different gifts for doing certain things well. So if God has given you the ability to prophesy, speak out with as much faith as God has given you. If your gift is serving others, serve them well. If you are a teacher, teach well. If your gift is to encourage others, be encouraging. If it is giving, give generously. If God has given you leadership ability, take the responsibility seriously. And if you have a gift for showing kindness to others, do it gladly. (Romans 12:6–8 NLT)

Reflection

*Write about some things that are unique to you
and how they add color to the world around you.*

Journal

You might twirl into life
with joyful pirouettes,
but it's the leaps that
prove you love the dance.

—Josiah Cullen

DAY 19

Re-choice and Rejoice

By Tahni Cullen

H as anyone dared you to do something exhilarating and terrifying?

After I gave my talk at a women's retreat, seven of us new acquaintances retired to a cozy fireside room. One nicely matching fortysomething blonde, a Midwest stay-at-home mom who admitted to being "kind of uptight," told a story of a dancer friend she met at church.

This eclectic seventy-five-year-old woman had trained at prestigious New York dance schools and traveled the world with a Christian dance troop. Expressive and wild-eyed, the dancer was drawn to the reserved mom, despite the mom's best attempts to dodge her.

As months went by, the unlikely duo became best friends, and one day the dancer coaxed the mom to let loose and try twirling. According to the mom, "She told me that in Hebrew the word *rejoice* in Scripture meant to 'spin around with emotion.' So she clapped, 'C'mon girl, twirl and see what rejoicing feels like!'"

That day, the mom leapt and twirled, and like King David, she didn't care how undignified she appeared. Something inside broke free, and she didn't look back.

Sometimes God sends a gift of new courage through someone who isn't like you. If that person dares you to dance your dance, why not keep an open posture and watch God release more freedom?

Meditation

But let all those rejoice who put their trust in You;
Let them ever shout for joy, because You defend
   them;
Let those also who love Your name
Be joyful in You. (Psalm 5:11 NKJV)

You did it: you changed wild lament
   into whirling dance;
You ripped off my black mourning band
   and decked me with wildflowers.
I'm about to burst with song;
   I can't keep quiet about you.
GOD, MY GOD,
   I can't thank you enough. (Psalm 30:11–12 MSG)

Reflection

*Recall how a person in your past or present
influenced you to do something you didn't think
you could or would do. How did that
experience change you?*

Journal

Journal

I need bigger joy.
I need greater love.
I need higher peace.
I need very big rights.
I'm so giving inside.
My heart can't take it
    anymore.
I need my God to soar.

—Josiah Cullen

DAY 20

True Needs

By Cheryl Ricker

Tahni and I are always amazed at Josiah's strong sense of self-awareness. That boy is more in tune with his gifts, callings, and abilities than most adults. He knows his weaknesses and strengths, and he knows the gifts he needs to value most: gifts that keep on giving. Gifts like greater love, bigger joy, and higher peace.

More importantly, Josiah knows where these gifts come from. They are from the one who helps us spread our wings like high-flying eagles.

Notice how Josiah thinks of his "rights" differently than the rest of the world? He wants to give until his heart explodes with joy. Who thinks like that? When most of us think of our "rights," we think of what we deserve for ourselves.

The truth is, however, that none of us deserves God's good gifts. We especially don't deserve God's greatest gift, himself. God gives us the right to be called children of God. When we say yes to Jesus, he comes alongside us in every situation, and by his Spirit, he infuses us with everything we need to be more like him.

Meditation

Yet to all who did receive him, to those who believed in his name, he gave the right to become children of God. (John 1:12 NIV)

But those who trust in the LORD will find new
    strength.
    They will soar high on wings like eagles.
They will run and not grow weary.
    They will walk and not faint. (Isaiah 40:31 NLT)

Therefore I remind you to stir up the gift of God which is in you through the laying on of my hands. For God has not given us a spirit of fear, but of power and of love and of a sound mind. (2 Timothy 1:6–7 NKJV)

Reflection

*What gifts did Jesus give you
the first time you said yes to him?*

*If you've never said yes to Jesus, write out
a simple prayer to him, asking him to be a bigger
part of your life. He wants to be your friend.*

Journal

Journal

Picture a gift to be given to you by opening your hands.
Picture a gift to be found by you by opening your eyes.
Lay up your treasure in heaven like it says by first learning to treasure what God has laid out for you on earth.

—Josiah Cullen

DAY 21

Art-A-Whirl

By Josiah Cullen

Art-A-Whirl in Minneapolis was my reality check. It was my aim to put all my fears aside and go see art mapped out all over the place in little studios of desire.

It was my joy to go into big brick buildings and go up staircases to see art in many forms. Readiness lit up my face, but my anxious ways wanted to mope. If less was more, my more insisted on reaching a limit and just picking a first-lit exit sign, allowing me to picture laws again. It made me think I'm not strong enough to live inside of the gifts I see.

Yet, my safe mom and dad said it would be great to look at just one more studio's artful display. It was like stars opened up, and strength inspired me to ring a bell to gifts of hours in art.

The Good Gift Giver

We value our Gift Giver more than his gifts. He is the one to rave about, but art is so much like my Papa's gifts. Gifts are so artful and rich inside of us, yet we need to remain in the studios and not leave like our senses tell us to. We need just to stay.

Meditation

"Yes, I am the vine; you are the branches. Those who remain in me, and I in them, will produce much fruit. For apart from me you can do nothing." (John 15:5 NLT)

But that doesn't mean you should all look and speak and act the same. Out of the generosity of Christ, each of us is given his own gift. The text for this is,

> He climbed the high mountain,
> He captured the enemy and seized the booty,
> He handed it all out in gifts to the people.

(Ephesians 4:7–8 MSG)

Every good gift and every perfect gift is from above, and comes down from the Father of lights, with whom there is no variation or shadow of turning. (James 1:17 NKJV)

Reflection

When are you most afraid to embrace
the beautiful plan God has for your life?
What step can you take to open your eyes
and hands to the joy-filled hidden gifts he
wants his brave seekers to find?

Journal

Our Father

Adapted from Matthew 6:9–13
by Josiah Cullen

My Father is in my heaven, and I'm okay.

My joy is in his holiness.

Papa is holy.

His kingdom has come.

His mighty joy in my earth will be done.

Give me my love in holding me tight.

Place my long meal of love in our plant of growth.

Please forgive my painful panting for man's desires.

Please don't mind those who painfully put me aside in
their love.

Safety is in your kingdom.

And power is in your glory forever.

Until I'm with you in heaven for good.

About the Authors

Tahni Cullen is a people-lover, blogger, and conference speaker who brings a powerful message of hope and restoration. Tahni worked for thirteen years at a multi-campus church in the Twin Cities of Minnesota, serving in communication arts and as a ministry director. She is a freelance marketer and performs in an original live variety show for women's events. Tahni and her producer husband, Joe, have created an award-winning documentary called *Surprised by Autism*. They live with their son, Josiah, in Saint Paul, where they enjoy exploring Minnesota's museums and destinations.

Eleven-year-old **Josiah Cullen** uses an iPad as his voice. His poetry and thought-provoking quotes about God's love enable him to connect with others through his Facebook page, *Josiah's Fire*. Josiah attends an autism school and enjoys family outings to sensory-friendly movies, plays, and concerts for people with special needs. And he likes climbing, jumping, and playing with his dog, Lucy.

 **Cheryl Ricker** is an author, blogger, speaker, and poet who enjoys all things artsy. She writes supernatural true-life stories that ignite people's passion to pursue God. Like *Josiah's Fire*, her first book of this genre, *Rush of Heaven: One Woman's Miraculous Encounter with Jesus*, also reveals that with God all things are possible. Cheryl studied creative writing at York University in Toronto, Ontario, and theology at Christ for the Nations Institute in Dallas, Texas. When Cheryl is not writing books, painting with watercolors, or sharing her faith, she loves having heart-to-heart conversations with her husband and two sons at their home in southeast Minnesota.

Josiah's Fire

Autism Stole His Words, God Gave Him a Voice

TAHNI CULLEN with Cheryl Ricker

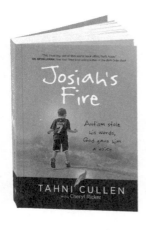

First-time parents Joe and Tahni Cullen were thrust into the confusing world of autism when their toddler, Josiah, suddenly lost his ability to speak, play, and socialize. The diagnosis: Autism Spectrum Disorder. In their attempts to see Josiah recover and regain speech, the Cullens underwent overwhelming physical, emotional, and financial struggles. While other kids around him improved, Josiah only got worse.

Five years later, Josiah, who had not been formally taught to read or write, suddenly began to type on his iPad profound paragraphs about God, science, history, business, music, strangers, and heaven. Josiah's eye-opening visions, heavenly encounters, and supernatural experiences forced his family out of their comfort zone and predictable theology, catapulting them into a mind-blowing love-encounter with Jesus.

- Find hope in hardship.
- Catch a fresh glimpse of heaven.
- Learn to hear and trust God's voice.
- Identify the roles of Father, Son, and Spirit.
- Be aware of the workings of angels, and much more!

Follow a trail of truth into Josiah's mysterious world, and see why his family and friends can no longer stay silent.

JosiahsFire.com